Digitizing Microfilm and Microfiche

Ronald J. Leach

Published by AfterMath, 2024.

While every precaution has been taken in the preparation of this book, the publisher assumes no responsibility for errors or omissions, or for damages resulting from the use of the information contained herein.

DIGITIZING MICROFILM AND MICROFICHE

First edition. February 28, 2024.

ISBN: 979-8224660889

Written by Ronald J. Leach.

Also by Ronald J. Leach

Software Reuse: Methods, Models, Costs, Second Edition
Why 2K?
Where Have All The Templars Gone?
User Guide to Microfilm and Microfiche
The 101 Most Important UNIX and Linux Commands
Baltimore Blue and Freddie Gray
Digitizing Microfilm and Microfiche
Managing a Digital Estate Without Paper Records

Table of Contents

Introduction

This book is intended for the person or persons with organizational responsibility for making an existing wealth of information currently on microfilm or microfiche available to users and for making sure that this wealth of information is preserved over time for future users. A reader whose primary interest is in being a user of microfilm or microfiche should read the author's *Users Guide to Microfilm and Microfiche,* also published as an ebook by AfterMath. Most of the discussion here will be be focused on digitization of the far more common microfilm, with digitization of microfiche discussed as necessary.

Of course, many organizations with extremely large amounts of microfilm and microfiche data have completed, or are well under way in the process of digitizing records. Think of the National Archives, for example. This book is likely to be most useful to much smaller organizations, with far less data, and certainly a much smaller budget. Of course, anyone can learn from the experiences of large digitization projects, both successful and not, and tailor the lessons learned to fit a particular organizational need.

You might wonder why an entire book is devoted to microfilm and microfiche, when so much genealogical, historical, and other archival information already has been digitized and is available on the Internet. Like many organizations, large and small, your organization has either already begun, or completed, the process of digitization of all of your records stored on microfilm of microfiche, or at least it is considering the possibility. So why do you need this book? There are several reasons.

First, a huge amount of information is available only on microfilm and microfiche, and this will remain the case for many, many years. Second, a large portion of the material on the Internet, particularly material created by the efforts of enthusiastic family historians beginning their genealogy studies, is of lesser quality, or has lesser overall importance, than what is available on microfilm rolls and microfiches that were created by government agencies, newspapers, or historical societies.

Both curators and users of microfilm and microfiche are probably aware that, rather than keep rooms full of flammable paper, many libraries have archived copies of newspapers only on microfilm or microfiche. Some older libraries, particularly smaller, specialized ones, have their catalogs available only on microfiche.

Unfortunately, microfilm and microfiche readers take up a considerable amount of room, not to mention the space needed to house the cabinets and shelves needed to store the microfilm rolls, themselves. The picture shown in Figure 1 below shows just how much precious space can be required for public storage of microfilm. The image shows a tiny amount of what is stored just on microfilm alone at a single local Family History Library Center, operated by the Church of Latter Day Saints (the Mormons).

Figure 1. Storing microfilm requires space!

Experienced curators of microfilm probably know that the situation is worse than it appears. Users, even the careful ones, cause wear and tear on the actual microfilm tapes. Threading a microfilm tape leader through a set of rollers and under a simple piece of glass used as a weight to hold microfilm images in focus causes minute amounts of abrasion, which can add up over time. Users who are less than careful can, of course, cause even more damage. For this reason, many organizations have one or more duplicate sets of tapes that are used in reserve, kept off limits to the general public. The duplicate microfilm tapes can be stored in relatively compact, less elaborate containers, but they still require some space and reasonable environmental conditions.

In addition, there are special lamps and cleaners needed for the microfilm and microfiche readers. Duplicate lamps are needed. As technology moves on, the cables connecting these microfilm and microfiche readers to printers become obsolete, because printer technology and communications technology change as well. Most libraries and similar institutions have replaced original printers that had parallel ports, first by printers with serial ports, then by printers with FireWire ports, then by printers with USB ports, then by printers with wired Ethernet connections to a local area network (LAN), then by WiFi connections, and so on.

Many microfilm readers are bulky, as can be seen from the image shown in Figure 2 below.

Figure 2. A typical microfilm reader.

The Difference Between Microfilm and Microfiche

What's the difference between microfilm and microfiche? As indicated above, microfilm is almost always available in reels, whose contents are seen by loading one end of a tape into a microfilm reader conveying the original reel onto a take-up reel.

Microfiche is different. It almost always comes on sheets that lie flat in order to go through a microfiche reader. Figure 3 shows a typical microfiche sheet and a box that that acts as a typical microfiche holder is shown in Figure 4.

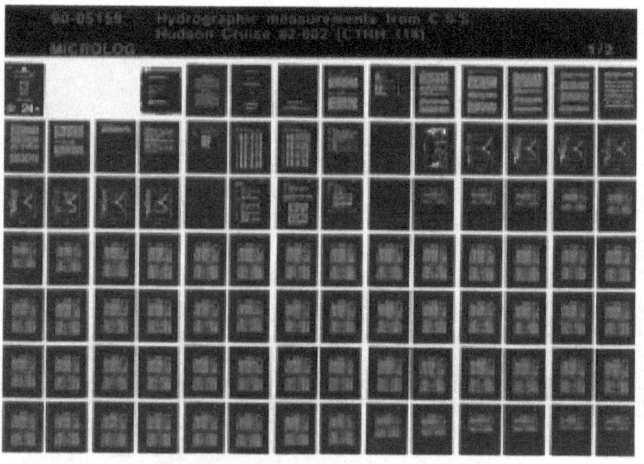

Figure 3. A typical microfiche sheet.

Figure 4. A typical microfiche holder.

There are also somewhat hidden differences between microfilm and microfiche that can affect the prioritizing of any digitization project. The most common substrate used for storing microfiche is more likely to deteriorate than what is typically used for microfilm, so microfiche assets should probably be digitized first. An extremely valuable web page on the National Archives website has more information. Search for archives.gov/preservation/formats, and then click on the page labeled "microfilm and microfiche" for details.

We note in passing that the National Archives provides the ability to purchase copies of microfilm on its main page.

Has Your Data Been Digitized Already ?

It appears to be appealing to have all data digitized. How universal is this belief? There are "digital history projects" at numerous universities, archives, and professional societies. The availability of digital archives, such as the *Wayback Machine* hosted by the essential *Internet Archive* at www.archive.org[1], makes it easy to imagine a day when all essential data published on the web will be

---

1. http://www.archive.org

available forever. (The *Wayback Machine* is privately funded through donations and is **not** a service of the United States Government.).

The existence of the *Wayback Machine* helps insure that a critical website containing essential information, such as a government archive, can never have all its information destroyed by, say, malicious vandalism, or operator error. It is certainly possible that some of the digitized data that your organization has might be available on the *Wayback Machine*. It doesn't hurt to check. Some sort of a snapshot of the contents of an important website, say, one with irreplaceable scientific research data, is intended to always be available, subject to the limitations of coverage by the *Wayback Machine*.

Archives as big as the *Wayback Machine* are almost certainly set up as a cloud. We use the term "cloud" in its most common form in the computer industry, where storing information in "the cloud" means that you as a creator or user don't have to know specifically which server contains your data. The software that manages "the cloud" keeps track of what specific data is stored where, just where that collection of data is actually stored on, say, server X, and a search engine will search that specific server X. That's the same way that Amazon Cloud Services, Google Cloud, Apple iCloud, etc. are organized. If you store your personal photos in "the cloud," you don't know specifically which server has the photos, and it doesn't matter —you probably just care that you can get access to them whenever you want.

It is probably a good idea for you to think about using a cloud once you have completed at least a significant portion of your digitation project. Once your organization has a large set of digital assets, it may chose to have all of them stored on computer servers in house, which probably requires access to technical staff to run them, or else store them store them somewhere in a cloud, which may be managed by a cloud service and, therefore, cost money. Also, there may be additional monetary concerns, because many institutions depend on membership dues or user fees to help pay their bills.

We won't focus on these general, industry-wide, digital preservation issues in this book. Instead, we will describe the types of resources, both financial and otherwise, that are necessary for any digital conversion project, regardless of the approach used. Both long-term and short-term financial issues of digitization will be discussed. Ideally, all the information presented here will guide you towards the solution that is best for your organization. Keep in mind the old adage "if it ain't broke, don't fix it." Remember that, unless your organization has had a major disaster, such as a fire, earthquake, or building collapse, your current system is working to some degree, probably even well enough for many of your users.

My Experiences With Microfilm and Microfiche

I have to admit that I was surprised when I first realized that what had been three sections in an earlier genealogy book I wrote became two books just on the subject of microfilm and microfiche. Certainly, when I spent my summers as an intern working in quality control and analysis of microfilmed documents at the Social Security Administration in Woodlawn, Maryland during the early 1960s, I never thought I would have to work with microfilm again, much less write a book on the subject. Little did I know.

Here's a brief overview of my experience with microfilm since my days at Social Security. As an amateur genealogist studying my family history I used microfilm and microfiche many times in various historical societies, libraries, and governmental archives.

I worked on microfilm digitization and analysis for records of the Freedmen's Bureau at Howard University, supporting the Freedmen's Bureau Record Preservation Act of 2000 with generous support from Microsoft.

I worked on two transcription projects, involving digitization of funeral home records for two local historical societies, as well as coordinating a digitization project with microfilming sets of local newspapers for yet another local society.

I also supervised a project to link existing microfilm records with a non-profit organization that wish to integrate its locally developed "finding aids" using the Z39.50 protocol for coordination with an ongoing digitization effort. This protocol is formally known as International Standard, ISO 23950: "Information Retrieval (Z39.50): Application Service Definition and Protocol Specification."

(There are many systems intended for use by small libraries that use Z39.50 and similar protocols. A recent search for the phrase "software for small libraries" lists about 2,650,000 hits. Among them is a list of "10 top companies" on the capterra.com website.)

I have had many conversations about digital preservation with an expert at the branch location of the National Archives at College Park, Maryland (known colloquially as Archives II).

And, of course, I spent many hours using microfilm records for my research into my family and my wife's family histories. This effort was fun, even though some called it "ancestor worship" and others called it "trivial pursuit."

Organization of This Book

This book contains eight chapters and an appendix that are organized as follows.

In Chapter 1, we describe the importance of understanding technical obsolescence and how the risk of it can be minimized.

Chapter 2 discusses the fundamental question of whether digital images can replace analog records such as those provided on microfilm and microfiche.

Chapter 3 provides a brief overview of the options available for digitization of microfilm and microfiche. Briefly speaking, the approaches are buy or lease a previously digitized product, buy or lease a professional digitization service that is performed either remotely or on-site, or perform the digitization using your own organization's personnel, after they have been trained in digitization, either on leased or purchased digitization equipment, and either on-site or remotely. It is expected that you will find one of more of these digitization approaches suitable for your organization's needs among these listed options.

In order to develop a plan for your digitization efforts, you must do an assessment of your organization's assets and liabilities first. In Chapter 4, we discuss what must go into an assessment process for such a digitization effort. The planning effort, economic issues, and project management issues involved in using each of these types of approaches to digitization will be discussed in separate chapters.

Chapter 5 describes the planning, economic, and and implementation issues for either buying or renting a previously digitized product that meets your organization's needs. Both short-term and long-term issues for this digitization effort will be discussed.

Chapter 6 describes the planning, economic, and implementation issues if your organization buys or leases a professional digitization service, whether the digitization is performed either remotely or on-site.

Chapter 7 describes the planning, economic, and implementation issues if your organization performs the digitization using its own personnel or volunteers, after they have had at least some minimal training in digitization, either on rented or purchased digitization equipment or, in rare cases, by using equipment from another organization.

Finally, Chapter 8 considers several possible long-term strategies for preventing digital obsolescence.

The single Appendix contains links to downloadable spreadsheets that can be used to provide templates for economic analysis and planning purposes, or for project management.

Chapter 1. Technological Obsolescence

In one sense, microfilm and microfiche are immune to technological obsolescence. The design of a microfilm reader is simple — it basically consists of a light, a lens that is focusable; a mechanism for advancing, rewinding, and storing tapes of microfilm, and a box to contain the essential tapes. This technology is likely to work for a long time, regardless of technological change - assuming the equipment doesn't break and you can find replacement parts, just as long as the microfilm tape isn't so abraded that the images on it are no longer visible. Even if a tape is broken due to extensive wear, its ends can always be spliced together. In the worst case scenario, each individual image can be magnified. No computer obsolescence is involved except for a user storing specific images on an attached printer, a personal USB or similar storage device.

Software technology changes, too, and the changes are often hard to see from outside For example, Macintosh computers currently use a standard Apple application called Preview instead of the common PDF Reader, and the PDF Writer software from Adobe that are extremely common on Windows-based PCs. Apple claimed at one time that Adobe's PDF software had some vulnerability to hacking. I won't comment on that issue, because it was so long ago that it probably doesn't matter any longer. Probably! Any long-time user of *Microsoft Word* has seen incompatibility issues with different versions of that software. Try to open a file that was created ten or more years ago. Or try to open a new file with old software.

Here's an example of a painful experience I had due to a technology obsolescence problem. I did have problems just with Adobe PDF Writer at the worst possible time. During my last year as a Professor of Computer Science, I was the lead scientist on my university's portion of a major multi-university project proposal with two large industrial partners for what were called secondary uses of electronic health records. The deadline was fast approaching and a series of three major snowstorms was predicted for the Washington, D.C. area in the next two weeks. The snow was coming fast that day and I expected a difficult and dangerous commute home from my office.

I used my office desktop computer to create the PDF file that the NIH (National Institutes of Health) required to be submitted on grants.gov[1]. I saved the file to a flash drive and then created a series of on-line assignments to load onto my university's content management system, because I knew neither my students nor I could afford two weeks of idle time. There were no capability for zoom calls or similar to be available in those days, so I used the same flash drive to load lectures and assignments. I packed up my briefcase and started home, ready for the long commute. Nearly two hours later. I was halfway home and remembered that I'd left the flash drive on my desk! I figured I could still get the grant in on time if I worked on an earlier version of the grant proposal that I had at home.

The educational material for my students was no problem because I had remote access, just a lot of work. Getting the big proposal to the grants.gov[2] portal was harder, because that site would only allow any portion of a proposal to be worked on when all earlier portions were complete. I had an old version of PDF Writer at home, and I was fortunate to finally get the NIH proposal through all the consistency checks the software required.

I called a helpful colleague in our Office of Research Administration and, even though the university was officially closed, he was able to read the proposal and access the grants.gov[3] portal, a week ahead of the deadline. Many thanks to him!

Then the disaster hit. The NIH portal software stated that the proposal format was not consistent with the form required. I got my colleague to explain to the university's director of the Office of Research Administration and we got an extension, possibly because the federal government was closed during much of the two week Snowmageddon. I got back to my office and submitted the proposal using the computer there. It went through easily and was reviewed.

What was the problem? The two versions of Adobe PDF Writer had small incompatibilities that were ignored by the software on grants.gov[4] used for validation of new proposals, but were fatal when the actual process of evaluation of evaluation started.

---

1.   http://grants.gov

2.   http://grants.gov

3.   http://grants.gov

4.   http://grants.gov

This type of incompatibility is extremely worrisome to many digital archivists, because this means that maintaining many versions of essential software may be expensive.The digital archive community has been working on this problem for many years. Just keep in mind that all you need to read a roll of microfilm is a magnifying glass.

It might seem that microfilm and microfiche are totally insulated against the possibility of either hardware or software obsolescence. Not true. Bulbs, cables, lenses, unavailability of parts, ancient software to print — changes to any of these things, or even discontinuation, might make your display and control devices obsolete

There is another kind of obsolescence besides the likelihood of possible changes to computers and software — deterioration of media. A photographic image stored on acid-free paper and stored aways from light, will probably always be usable during our lifetimes, because it could be photographed and the resulting image enhanced.

Microfilm and microfiche have a special kind of obsolescence. The medium itself may deteriorate. The material most commonly used for the carrier of the microfilm and the material most commonly used as the carrier of the microfiche have different expected life spans, with microfiche the most endangered, so it is probably best to digitize your organization's microfiche assets first. (The National Archives is well aware of this and indicates the methods of preserving these assets on its aforementioned webpages.)

Microfiche is highly susceptible to environmental conditions, especially involving ionized air (which may create ozone) within rooms that have microfiche. Again, see the section on preservation in the aforementioned National Archives website for more information.

We now turn to the discussion of the specific types of analog formats that may be candidates for digitization within your organization.

Microfilm

Microfilm has a somewhat hidden advantage over digital media from a data integrity perspective. It is intended to be be read sequentially, so it is easy to determine if a particular image has been deliberately removed or inserted, affecting the historical accuracy of the tape's contents. Making the same determination for digital images may require significant computer forensic analysis.

Every organization tries to have the latest, most useful, technology, subject to budgetary and staffing limitations. Even so, there is a constant concern that a technology that is pervasive now may not be easily accessible later, or not even available at all. Think about the hardware technologies that are hard or even impossible to find today: magnetic tape cassettes, 8-inch floppy disks, 5.25-inch floppy disks, 3.5-inch floppy disks, 2-inch floppy disks, zip drives, CDs, and DVDs. Even a technology that worked on one of these storage media on a PC might not have worked on a Mac or vice-versa. Formats of files may change. Could technology obsolescence happen to a microfilm reader or printer?

Here's the approximate state of affairs in the area of microfilm preservation as it is viewed by the National Archives.

Microfilm that was created using the expensive silver halide (usually silver iodide) process, with the images stored in a gelatin emulsion that is stored on the reels, has been estimated to have an archival life of 500 years. Unfortunately, the gelatin emulsion does not do well in damp, warm climates, so there are difficulties if a HVAC system fails or even degenerates over time. Places such as the National Archives invest a considerable amount of effort to make certain that environmental conditions are within very strict guidelines, with multiple backup systems.

Many organizations use microfilm rolls created using much cheaper processes, and, therefore, with a much shorter expected useful life, simply plan to replace these rolls on a regular basis.

We note that the aforementioned National Archives website has advice for repairing microfilm. One critical major recommendation is to not use tape (of the kind typically found in office supply stores) to splice broken microfilm reels. See that website for more information.

Microfiche

Like microfilm, microfiche is a technology medium for storing images of documents in highly condensed form. The term "microfiche" is also used to describe the process of creating this type of storage. A standard microfiche is a flat, relatively rigid, piece of plastic, with dimensions 105 x 148 millimeters, which is not much larger than a standard 4 inch by-6 inch index card for those readers who are not comfortable with metric system measurements. As with microfilm, a microfiche sheet is inserted into a special reader. Since microfiche has a fixed size and is also flat, the feed mechanism is much narrower than that required for microfilm, since there is no need for any space needed to accommodate the roll of microfilm to travel, winding its way from the original microfilm reel to the take-up reel on the other side of the reader's lens.

A microfiche reader is even simpler than a microfilm reader; at least in theory. It doesn't even require a mechanism for advancing, rewinding, and storing tapes. All it really needs is a magnifier that has a high degree of magnification. Of course, microfiche is usually embedded in sheets, and, as anyone ever had to manage an organization that uses microfiche knows, microfiche sheets can be placed in the wrong envelopes and easily can be lost. Microfiche sheets can even be stolen.

Some archives will display microfiche in file cabinets that are specially sized for microfiche storage. Others, especially if they are relatively small and have little of their valuable collection copied to microfiche, may have the collection stored in loose-leaf notebooks with sleeves for the individual microfiche sheets. In many libraries and archives, the microfiche sheets may not be directly accessible by users and, therefore, have to be requested by users. We will discuss this issue in more detail when we consider microfiche etiquette.

There are a few differences between microfiche and microfilm that you should be aware of. There are four possible orientations of a microfiche sheet, so users may have to turn the plastic around several times before they get it right. They can even be inserted backwards! That's a total of eight possible orientations, with seven being erroneous.The possibility of such an inadvertent change of orientation may require a presort before digitization begins.

The magnification is so high that a fingerprint will not cause anywhere near as much damage as it might on a tape containing microfilm.Ideally, a user of microfiche will remember that microfiches are very easy to misplace and will follow the directions of the organization where he or she is reviewing the microfiche to avoid any problems.

Chapter 2. Can Digital Images Replace Analog?

We use the term "analog" to refer to images that can be read either directly or by a magnifying device alone, such as microfilm and microfiche. In one sense, the question is ridiculous, because microfilm and microfiche have different physical forms. In reality, the more important question is whether a digital image accurately reflects the contents of the microfilm or microfiche images it was created from. Equally important, will the digital image continue to reflect these contents as technology changes and document format standards change?

Change of Viewpoint

In order to have the digitization achieve its greatest utility to your organization's users (who are your customers) it is critical to change your perspective from considering how users access data currently on microfilm to how they will search for it digitally. We'll start with microfilm first.

The example of digitizing a run of newspapers illustrates the simplest case of how our viewpoint has to change. A complete run of microfilm reels for, say ten years, of weekly issues of a hypothetical newspaper, may consist of ten reels that are labeled something like *Kalamazoo Citizen 1900, Kalamazoo Citizen 1901, ... Kalamazoo Citizen 1909.* These labels can be thought of as naming ten digitized files, each of which is placed in a single directory named something like *Kalamazoo Citizen 1900-1909.* This simple type of naming convention can be extended if, say, more reels of this hypothetical newspaper become available. The term "naming is commonly used in the digitization industry.

A user wishing to search microfilm records for a particular article that first appeared on a particular date will select the appropriate reel for that year, insert it into a microfilm reader, thread it through the lens mechanism to a take-up reel, then advance the microfilm reel, scrolling through the images until the proper date will be found. Users will speed up or slow down the scrolling, depending on where they think the image shown on the microfilm reader is relative to the date they are searching for. They may go through several tries, moving the reel forward or backward, until they find the newspaper issue with the desired date. They will then examine that issue for the information they want.

The search of any set of digitized data certainly will be different. Regardless of what type of local search engine capability is available, most modern search engines that exist today will be able to be search most computer servers, regardless of the nature of the searches. The search will be done directly, in the sense that the user will go to a particular issue in what appears to be a single effort, perhaps finding a specific month, or even a specific year.. This ubiquitous search ability will certainly not decrease in the future.

It is also important to keep in mind that a user probably doesn't want to to keep their finger on an arrow key for a long period, but might prefer some bookmarks indicating a month. Therefore, being able to start a digital search in the appropriate month is advantageous. That probably means a new file for each month, perhaps, even for each week. Unfortunately, such fine-grained searching comes at a cost in both time and money.

This means that, in effect, the data for this run of newspaper issues is grouped together by months, and appears to a typical user to be stored in different folders on a computer. Use of the digitized data can be made much easier by effectively inserting a place holder.

How is this finer-grained searching enabled? This can be done mechanically on microfilm, using one of two destructive methods: either by cutting the tape and inserting a piece of tape with the single image of the name of the month, or by separating the tape for a year into twelve tapes.

This destructive approach has another disadvantage A digitized version of an altered microfilm roll doesn't have the same level of being authoritative as a the original microfilmed data. Think of of the "chain of evidence" procedures of any police procedural drama on television.

There is a second, non-destructive method to enable finer searching. A far better approach is to determine the month boundaries, either using human or digital determination and inserting twelve single-page images.

Most digitization companies describe this latter, non-destructive approach as "naming," and it will often be part of a digitization effort.

This type of naming issue described above is not generally a problem for microfiche data. Microfiche sheets typically contain a much smaller amount of data than standard microfilm rolls. The individual sheets are labeled with a title. The sheets themselves are contained in labeled envelopes. These sets of labels are the most likely ones to serve as file names.

One last thing needs to be mentioned. Digitizing a document that was on microfilm or microfiche just allows viewing it. Location of specific names within a set of digitized images will require optical character recognition software, or OCR. A discussion of OCR is beyond the scope of this book.

Protection Against AI

The unexpected ability of artificial intelligence engines such as ChatGPT to understand and create many complex documents has caused great concern about data integrity among many people. AI-based systems can make it hard to distinguish accurate information from sources that may contain incorrect information from those with accurate information.

It is also possible that data can be deliberately changed to contain fraudulent information. If the legal validity of archival records, such as birth, marriage, and divorce certificates becomes questioned, chaos can occur. The same is true for records of trials of various medicines and treatments.

The potential for possible errors in medical diagnosis is also worrisome. The United States federal standards law known as HIPAA (Health Insurance Portability and Affordability Act) provides some assurance of data security, but there is always a possibility of tampering.

While it is certainly impossible to turn back the clock on increased usage of AI, it will become increasingly important to have a non-digital, purely analog source of information that is as reliable as it was at the time it was created. Everyone knows about the large number of fake videos and photographs that are increasingly pervasive online. The National Archives current approaches to data security protect against this by using a highly secure cloud using Department of Defense capabilities.

Of course, most curators of archival information are well aware of this, and make efforts to have archival data stored as read-only. Still, computers can be hacked, and not every organization's resources allow the possibility of using a highly secure cloud.

Keeping analog images, such as read-only images of newspapers and state and local archives is essential.

Chapter 3. Overview of Digitization Options

Once digitization is being considered, questions arise as how to do it, how long will it take, and at what cost. The best way to address them is to consider the basic options like any other technology project, using roughly the following categories to determine how to proceed with the digitization:

- Buy an already digitized product.
- Lease an already digitized product.
- Buy digitization service from a company.
- Lease digitization service from a company.
- Do-it-yourself digitization at your organization.
- Do nothing.

In the remainder of this chapter we'll discuss each of these alternatives briefly in turn. This will help with the assessment of the feasibility of the proposed digitization with the available resources, which we discuss in Chapter 4. This, in turn, precedes our discussion of the planning, economics, and actually carrying out the chosen approach to digitization that will be discussed in considerable detail in later chapter.

Buy or Lease A Previously Digitized Product

The **Buy an already digitized product** from a company option means that you find some organization that has already created the digital images of the microfilm or microfiche data that you wish to create and purchase the completed digitized product from them.

There are two variants of this strategy: buy the product as is without any changes, and buy the product with some configuration to make it work well with any existing searchable data your organization already has. We note that the most common type of configuration is in the area of what we have called "naming" in Chapter 2 previously.

The **Lease an already digitized product** from a service option means to obtain the use of the already digitized product for a fixed term as long as your organization pays the periodic rent. It is possible, even likely, that the monthly or yearly rental will go up after a preset term has expired. It is even possible that the company may go out of the digitization business or out of business entirely. This can have dire effects if the rental agreement is based on the digitizing company providing remote access to their servers instead of your organization's!

Buy Or Lease Digitization From A Service

The **Buy digitization from a service** option means to hire a service from a company that specializes in digitization for organizations of roughly the same size as yours. Of course, you must be sure that the company has the hardware, software, and technical support to do the digitization. The company will probably take your microfilm or microfiche to their own location and do the conversion at that location. Either you will specify the configuration issues in detail, or you will have to interact consistently with them.

Warning! Make sure that the company has a spotless reputation. You don't want to lose your precious data and get nothing in return if the company goes out of business.

The **lease digitization from a service** option means to lease the hardware and software, and obtain enough training to do the digitization work in house using your organization's existing staff. Consulting services will almost certainly be needed.

Do-It-Yourself Digitization

There are basically two different paths that can be followed if your organization decides to do the digitization primarily using internal resources.

The **Do-it-yourself** option means that your organization must find a place where a high quality digitizer is available but the digitization requires human attention. Several years ago, I used such a digitizer at a Mormon Church Family History Center in order to copy several years worth of a specialized newspaper for a local historical society. It took me about 60 hours of work to digitize ten years of issues. I was a volunteer, so this was a very low-cost approach. The hourly rental fee at the nearby Family History Center was nominal. (Not every local Family History Center has such a digitizing facility.)

A **hybrid approach** means using any standard, off-the-shelf hardware and software along with whatever hardware, software, and talent that you can find in or near your organization's locations and solve the problem that way. This may be the hardest approach to plan for.

Do Nothing

The **Do Nothing** approach is, obviously, to do no digitizing at all and keep the status quo. This is cheapest in the sense of no visible up-front cost, but may have consequences in terms of dissatisfied users, decreases in membership, or fewer drop-in users who are not members. It is, of course, hard to determine how many potential "customers" may be lost because of the perceived inconvenience of microfilm in a digitized world.

Each of the roughed-out digitization options that was briefly described above will be expanded upon considerably into specifically detailed options in the next three chapters.

As you can imagine, each of these approaches both has considerable advantages and disadvantages. I believe that the best strategy for anyone involved in the planning for a complex digitization project is to think about your organization's needs and capabilities for a bit, have a few conversations with colleagues, then turn to the next few chapters for a description of the planning and implementation issues, followed by economic assessments of each option. This approach will allow you (and your organization — it is highly unlikely that you will be making major decisions by yourself on a decision fraught with so many possible difficulties) to be able to plan for a successful digitization project.

Chapter 4. Assess the Feasibility of Digitization

The first step in any technology project, and digitization of microfilm and microfiche is certainly a technology project, is to take an inventory of what you have. You need to know the resources available.

A lot of things need to be considered for the planning and implementation of each of these approaches. In this chapter, we consider issues of budget, space, expected configuration of digitized data, quality standards, proposed new layout, person-hours needed from your organization, person-hours needed for external consultants, person-hours needed for staff training, time to implement, downtime when your data on microfilm or microfiche is not available to your customers, electrical power needs, new furniture, disposal of any old furniture and equipment, archival storage of existing microfilm and microfiche as backup, insurance needs.

In addition to the items listed above, your organization must decide how it wants to interact with both its current members (who are also customers) and how to grow the number of members. Will there be increased computing and networking capability in house, or will the data accessed be done remotely using a cloud-based design.

Once you have an approved, workable plan, you can consider the cost elements, which we will discuss in detail in Chapters 5 through 8.

The detailed inventory of items to be considered in your organization's plans should include the following as a minimum:

- Initial assessment of funds budgeted for this digitization effort. This initial budget estimate will certainly change over time.

- Short-term and long-term goals of the organization as to how it wants to use its access. This impacts both the way the organization expects to interact with digital users, and what, if any, existing space may become available for other purposes.

• Assessment of the availability and capability of staff to manage what may be a long-term effort.

• Assessment of the need for availability and training of staff to do the actual digitization if necessary.

• What standards will your organization require in the "naming" of data files created by the digitization process? Clearly, more naming means more cost.

• An assessment of patterns of use of existing microfilm and microfiche. Together with any surveys of frequent, infrequent, or organization members who have strongly indicated a desire for remote access, this will help provide guidance in planning what may be a rather expensive and tedious project.

• Complete descriptions of all existing microfilm and microfiche media. This should include the dates of each item in a series, with any missing microfilm reels or microfiche cards noted. This should be done for the microfilm and microfiche that is in regular use, as well as duplicate or backup media. Conditions should be noted if there is any obvious wear or damage.

• Examination of the inventory of microfilm and microfiche assets to determine if there are any duplicates. Any duplicates, including items intended as backups, should be counted. Deciding not to digitize duplicates can reduce the overall cost of the digitization project.

• Examination of the microfilm and microfiche assets to determine if any of the technology used to create them is currently obsolete. An example of such obsolescent technology is the way that searching the United States Census records has changed. At one time, finding a person's record in the census required using the Soundex coding of names, usually using a sheet that explains how to encode a surname into Soundex for further use. (Soundex is more than 100 years old. It was developed to help find names with variant spellings, such as

Smith, and Smythe.) Users then would consult an index (probably on microfilm) of the encoded name would be searched for a location of what is called an Enumeration District, or ED. Then the ED had to be searched for the desired person. Now, more advanced search techniques list a set of records in one step, even allowing for variations. Digitizing old microfilm records of the United States Census is simply not worth the effort.

• Complete descriptions of all microfilm and microfiche readers. The descriptions should list the manufacturer, the date the equipment was purchased, the connectivity type and status of each reader to printers (serial cable, parallel cable, FireWire, USB, USB-C, local printer, network printer, etc), whether a reader is still under warranty, and if so, the extent of such warranties.

• Complete descriptions of all printers used for printing for microfilm or microfiche readers. The descriptions should include the manufacturer, year, type of connection, availability of supplies, and likely obsolescence. The type of connection, such as serial cable, parallel cable, FireWire, USB, USB-C, etc., whether the reader is still under warranty, and if so, the extent of such warranties. Some printers have coin-operated controls; if so, they should be listed. (Many smaller libraries and archives use an honor system to charge for paper copies.)

• All relevant supplies and expendables. This includes bulbs for each type of microfilm or microfiche reader. Don't forget to include cables, power strips, lens cleaners, and even microfilm take-up spools and cards for insertion of sets of smaller microfiche.

• Tables, chairs, and other office furniture that can be repurposed for computers used for digitized materials.

• Complete assessment of space where the computers will be set up. The assessment should evaluate the quality of existing and proposed electrical service. It should be noted if conditioned power is available.

If not, the inventory should include the number and state of high-quality power strips with built-in circuit breakers.

• Complete assessment of what space can be gained by removing microfilm and microfiche readers as well as boxes of microfilm reels and microfiches.

• Complete assessment of the size and cost of storage areas that will have to be available during the digitization and afterward for redundancy. (Using such an area is often called "staging.")

• Complete assessment of any existing computers and Internet or internal intranet connectivity. This may include informal assessment of user's satisfaction with any existing services.

• Complete assessment of existing Internet connectivity status. This should be done if the newly digitized material is intended to be placed online for remote access. Staff technical expertise will need to be higher if sensitive data is to be made available on line. Any existing paywalls should be described.

• Will the newly digitized data be stored in a cloud?

• Will your organization increase its training of technical staff, or will it reduce staff in order to make use of a cloud service provider?

• Can digital images take the place as analog for your organization? As before, we use the term "analog" to refer to images that can be read by a magnifying device alone, such as microfilm and microfiche. In one sense, the question is ridiculous, because they have different physical forms. In reality, the more important question is whether a digital image accurately reflects the contents of the microfilm or microfiche images it was created from. Equally important, will the digital image continue to reflect these contents as technology changes and document format standards change. We'll expand upon this topic in the next chapter.

Legal Issues

Let's first consider the relationship of microfilm and microfiche images to the original paper documents from which they were created. For simplicity, we will ignore the situation when a microfilm image was taken of anything other than paper, such as a miniature picture of a physical object that was taken by a specialized device.

The standard reference for genealogical citations, Elizabeth Shown Mills' *Evidence Explained: Citing History Sources from Artifacts to Cyberspace*, indicates that a properly cited microfilm record from the United States Census is considered to be the equal of the original paper document in terms of authenticity. This is fortunate, since paper copies of most early census records have generally been removed from public access deliberately. This decision was motivated by the fact that nearly all the National Archives records for the 1890 United States were destroyed in a fire.

Many banks may keep microfilmed images of checks, even though they generally prefer their customers to go paperless. Why? Because they want an exact record.

Even prestigious colleges and universities, such as Williams College, still support microfilm and microfiche, simply because so much of their collection is only available in these forms.(See a recent article on the college website http://library.williams.edu/memex/2771 for an example.) The bottom line is that, for a large amount of historical and genealogical research you have to be able to read microfilm.

A critical question is, how much of your critical, irreplaceable data is available only on microfilm or microfiche? As we illustrated in Chapter 1 when we presented Figure 1, many large rooms are devoted to the storage and reading of microfilm.

Unfortunately, there is a serious negative to the replacement of microfilm readers with computerized images. A digital image is not precisely the same as the original analog image that was photographed onto the original microfilm roll. Even if no microfilm reader is available, images on a roll of microfilm can still be read using a magnifying glass. The same is true for images stored on microfiche.

Digital images may exist forever (unless there is a failure of a storage medium such as a hard disk), but the software needed to view them may change over time, making images difficult or impossible to read. This issue concerns many digital archivists, as does the issue of tampering by AI-based software intended to mislead. We will return to this issue in the last chapter of this book.

Data Security

This is often a problem for small organizations that cannot afford expensive labor costs to provide adequate computer security. Data that becomes unavailable is useless to your organization's users. Ransomeware is becoming easier for criminals to employ, and the only thing that keeps many of them away from many organizations is the likelihood that some potential targets are too small and have only limited resources to be attacked. Unfortunately, the problem is pervasive in society and there are no easy answers.

Perhaps the best approach for a small organization that is, at least, relatively simple, is to keep the archival data separate from the business side of the house as much as possible. This means, at the very least, separate computers, and, ideally, separate networks. Get the best technical computer help you can, and make sure that every decision about network design and data security is completely documented, so that there is at most minimal disruption in service if an attack occurs.

The suggestions made in the previous paragraphs may not be sufficient to provide adequate data security. What matters almost as much is whether your organization, or its most technologically knowledgeable leadership, believes it can or cannot protect online data properly. If the answer is that it cannot be protected, the data may still be digitized, but the servers holding the data, and the computers used to display it, may only be connected on a private network, and will not be available to potential remote users.

Separating the network with the data from the rest of your organization's computers greatly improves data security. It is highly unlikely that a potential data hacker will enter your organization's "back-of-the-house" physical location with a USB drive that contains hacking software. On the other hand, local computers in a publicly available room may be highly susceptible to a hacker with a simple USB drive. I know three people who were victims of a hack of a hotel computer that was intended to be used only to print boarding passes. Technicians can disable USB ports completely, or have them set to read only so that users can download data, but not upload anything.

The cost of this lockdown is, of course the barrier to remote users and this barrier may lead to reductions in the number of current or potential future members.

Intellectual Property

Perhaps your organization's primary asset is its intellectual property, which will be at increased risk of being compromised during any digitization process. Let's look at the possible vulnerabilities. Buying or leasing a previously digitized product from a reputable company, should be very safe, as long as your organization can be sure that it's users will be able to access the precious archives with minimal downtime during the transitional period when the new digital data is provided via computer and you have kept at least minimal ability to display microfilm or microfiche.

The risk to your intellectual property is increased, of course, if the digitization is done either outside your organization or by persons who are not familiar with the technology.

Current Microfilm Technology

The world has gone digital in most areas, and, even with the constant financial pressures, local historical societies, county and state archives centers, local and national Family History Centers, the National Archives, and public libraries all attempt to provide some level of digitization of their microfilm and microfiche reading capability.

Consequently, there have been many types of microfilm readers that have digitization capability.You may be familiar with some of the more common versions of such devices. Many such devices have the ability to have an entire roll of microfilm digitized, albeit at a rather slow pace. Other devices only digitize one image at a time, requiring the user to scroll through the microfilm roll by hand. A similar dichotomy holds for microfiche readers.

Figure 5 below shows a modern microfilm reader from *eImage Data* that occupies a rather small portion of a desktop. A standard computer monitor can be attached easily. A port on this device allows a computer to be attached, making the transfer of microfilm images to digital ones rather easy.

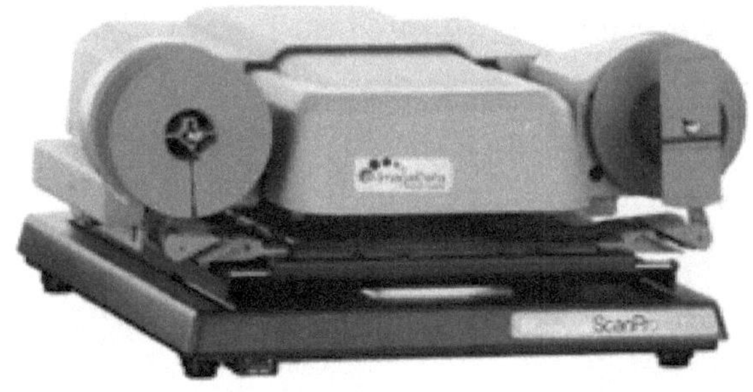

Figure 5. A small microfilm reader.

An image intended to indicate the size relative size of the same microfilm reader when connected to keyboard and a large, high-quality, high-resolution computer monitor is shown in Figure 6.

Figure 6. A modern microfilm reader connected
to a large, high-quality computer monitor.

There are several things to consider with essentially all these microfilm readers:

The first thing to consider is the speed of image transfer, which is a function of the number of images being transferred, can be extremely important in terms of the amount of technical labor involved in the transfer. Within each model in the current product line of nearly every vendor of microfilm readers, there is a direct correlation between price and speed of data transfer.

The second thing to consider is the amount of data transferred, which is a function of both the number of images transferred and the size of the images, is measured in bytes. As was the case with the speed of image transfer, within each model in the current product line of nearly every vendor of microfilm readers, there is a direct correlation between price and speed of data transfer. Too much data can overload computers and peripheral devices.

The third thing to consider is the quality of the digitized image, in comparison to the quality of the image on the microfilm, which is largely determined by the quality of the lenses, the automatic focusing mechanism, and the original images being digitized. As was the case with both the speed of image transfer and the amount of data transfer, within each model in the current product line of nearly every vendor of microfilm readers, there is a strong correlation between price and quality of the digitized image as well as the speed of image transfer and the speed of data transfer.

The first two observations are fairly obvious. It is important to note that there are two different actions going on during the transfer of images and these actions occur at different speeds. The first action is the turning of the microfilm reader's spool, which is considerably slower than the rate at which the second action of the data can be sent along, say, a USB cable, which is a rate that is often measured in megabits per second.

The third observation above requires additional information. If an image on the microfilm is improved by, say, making it sharper or improving contrast, a feature that is well-known by a user of Adobe Photoshop or similar products, additional time is needed in the processing of the images. The image processing time goes up, depending on the size of the image and the quality wanted. Since it may be critical for future archival research using the documents being filmed, it is essential to keep a copy reflecting of the exact images. This means that there will be at least *two* digital copies of each datum, one an exact replica, and the other, improved ones in general use.

Note that every roll of microfilm currently in use in an archive almost certainly will be stored in a box that has a standard size label describing the contents. There may be a label on the side of the microfilm spool reel itself, although this is not universal. If an entire microfilm roll is to be digitized at once, with all the digital images in the same file, then the digital file needs to be named before it is saved on the host computer or digital device. The name should be the same as the name of the microfilm roll's label.

I had to face these issues in a number of ways in other situations. As I mentioned previously, one historical society I worked with used a set of "finding aids" for describing locally stored records that were listed in the society's online searchable catalog. When some data was digitized, the information stored in these "finding aids" had to be merged with the existing online searchable catalog.

Current Microfiche Technology

In order to be consistent with the parallel structure in this book where we discuss both microfilm and microfiche issues in the same chapter we should describe the status of microfiche readers. Unfortunately, that would be more difficult than one might expect.

I have never been involved with digitizing data stored on microfiche and so I relied on a simple internet search for the term "microfiche reader" to get a sense of what equipment is available. I found many ads for used equipment on Amazon and eBay. The first thing I found from a direct website of a manufacturer of equipment led me to a company that has equipment that is what I would call "largely automated." That company provided support for several versions of PC- and Mac-hosted computers, but their hardware seemed to require pressing a foot pedal called a "footswitch" to copy each microfiche sheet.

I found a second company with a desktop solution that seems to require manual insertion of each sheet of microfiche. At that point, I stopped searching because I could see several things:

- There are only a few companies (at least compared to the number of companies that manufacture microfilm readers) that manufacture microfiche readers.

- There are many used microfiche readers available.

- The prices of used equipment for digitizing microfiche are low.

- The imaging market has already moved away from the transformation of microfiche. This is likely to be due to the well-known possibility of deterioration of microfiche sheets and the National Archives having prioritized the digitization of microfiche data.

Make of these conclusions what you will.

The Digitizing Options

Once the inventory assessment has been completed and there is a good understanding of what assets the organization has, it is time to move forward. For emphasis, the basic options for digitization are shown here

- Buy or lease a previously digitized product

- Buy or lease a digitization service with the digitization work done at the company's site

- Buy or lease a digitization service with the digitization company with the work done on-site using professionals

- Do-it-yourself digitization using purchased or leased equipment on-site

- Build the digitized product

- A combination of one or more of the above options

- Nothing

We'll discuss each of these ways in turn in the next few chapters.

Cloud Storage

We've mentioned the use of the cloud for data storage previously in this book. Now it is time for a closer look.

At first glance, it would seem to be easy to transfer all your digitized data to the cloud and also easy to reverse the process. Of course, a decision to move to the cloud has staffing, and perhaps internal political, issues. The cost of the hardware in the cloud <u>should</u> go down, but cloud fees are always subject to change.

Having a backup in the cloud is a good idea. Moving from one cloud service provider to another is relatively easy, but moving back all the data that your users are reading from your organization's data that was stored in the cloud to local storage may be difficult to implement if new staff must be hired. Use only cloud storage providers that you believe will remain in business.

There is no perfect answer. Make the best decision you can and live with it.

Chapter 5. Buy Or Lease A Previously Digitized Product

This chapter describes in detail the least risky method of digitization of your microfilm and microfiche data. This process has the least risk possible because your organization's data always remains under local control. There are possible problems, however, which is probably true in any contractual agreement.

Follow the suggestions here and you will be able to avoid nearly all problems.

What to Expect

First and foremost, you should expect the entity you are purchasing or leasing data from to have a complete and accurate description of the data under consideration. We use the term "entity" herein this chapter because, while the data is most likely to be purchased from a company that sells such data, it is possible to purchase the same data set from another organization that may be closing or selling off assets due to budgetary or other concerns.

Here is a list of the minimal things you should expect from any entity providing you with a complete set of data for purchase or lease.

- The entity must provide a complete and accurate description of the data they will be providing either for purchase or lease.

- The entity must provide assurance that they have the right to sell or lease the data.

- Rights to use must carry over to your organization.

- Any missing data must agree with what was indicated in the contract.

- The entity must provide the data by the time indicated in the contract.

- The entity must produce the data in the agreed-upon format.

- Instructions for delivery and installation must be provided.

- Technical support must be provided during the installation, if necessary.

- The cost of purchase must be provided for in the contract.

- The cost and terms of a lease must be provided for a leased product.

- Provisions of any lease-to-buy arrangement must be provided.

- The contract should specify if any provisions for your organization to retain the ability to purchase the data at a reduced payment if your organization misses a lease payment rather than pay full price.

- Any restrictions on the number of computer servers that can be used must be specified in the contract.

- Any restrictions on the number of concurrent users of the data must be specified in the contract.

- Are there discounts for purchasing more than one previously digitized product?

- Does the contract force your organization to purchase any other digitized product in the future?

- Does the provider of digitized data require being used as a sole source for any other data?

Planning for Digitization

At this point, your organization has decided that it is appropriate to consider digitizing some or all of its microfilm or microfiche. In our discussion, we'll assume that the potential for freeing up precious first-class space by removing microfilm and microfiche readers has been discussed, and that a less visible (and presumably far less expensive) location has been decided upon. Presumably, the potential impact in terms of ease of use for current patrons has been discussed, as has been the potential for new users.

A preliminary budget may have been developed. However, since such a budget projection is only a guess at this point, it is essential to specify the details of the product to be purchased or rented. For this step you will certainly need to follow an incremental process. I strongly suggest that you contact a set of digitization companies to get access to experienced representatives who can work with you in determining the scope of the needs of your organization. I have always found that the representatives will help with the process, at least at high level.

Beware of working with a company that uses a proprietary format for its data organization. Companies change and so do software standards. Whatever value that may be provided by a special formatting is much less important of having a standard that is not likely to become obsolete. A simple use of file format standards such as JPEG or PDF, through a typical browser-based search is likely to remain useful than a proprietary search mechanism. If given a choice, I suggest using the JPEG file format instead of PDF. At this point in time, all JPEG formats are backward compatible with the latest standards.

The first emphasis is on determining the scope of the digitization effort, which is usually measured in the number of spools of microfilm or, less often, sheets of microfiche. The spools of microfilm and sheets of microfiche generally are aggregated to make complete sets, such as years of issues of newspapers. It is important to determine if the product your organization wishes to purchase or lease consists of a complete run, such as the entire set of issues of a newspaper, or only a partial set Purchasing or renting from multiple sources may be necessary. If you use multiple sources, try to have the same naming conventions.

Once you have determined what you want digitized, it is necessary to specified how it it to be accessed. After all, your digitized data for this effort will have to be accessed via computer.

Let's reconsider a hypothetical digitization situation that we discussed in Chapter 2 where we stated that using names that make sense to most of your users is essential. As a reminder, in this example, there was a complete run of microfilm reels for ten years of weekly issues of a hypothetical newspaper, may consist of ten reels that are labeled something like *Kalamazoo Citizen 1900, Kalamazoo Citizen 1901, ... Kalamazoo Citizen 1909*. These labels can be thought of as naming ten digitized files, each of which is placed in a single directory named something like *Kalamazoo Citizen 1900-1909*. This simple type of naming convention can be extended if, say, more reels of this hypothetical newspaper become available.

Once you have determined the appropriate naming convention of how the how the digitized information will be stored and searched, it is time to move to the next planning step, which is planning the way your customers will access your newly digitized data. It is certainly easier to place all the data on a server, which is then accessed from computers (or just simple computer terminals in house) or, if we so choose, accessed from their homes. This requires a decision of whether or not a paywall must be established for users with remote access.

A more complicated situation might occur in, say land records or tax records. Nearly every state in the United States, and nearly every county (or parish in Louisiana) has had its boundaries changed multiple times since it was created.These boundary changes are almost certain to continue, and so will names of communities. This may, in fact, cause changes in file names and descriptions. Unfortunately, restrictions on the length of file names may vary on different computer operating systems, so there are stricter limits to names used on a computer beyond what can be written on the side of a box of microfilm, or on a piece of paper thumbtacked to a wall in a microfilm reading room. It really doesn't matter which option you choose, as long as the file names are not too long. However, you will need to be at least somewhat consistent in the naming conventions you use. Try to avoid file names that contain blanks.

Another, less common example, is the changes in spelling, possibly due to names of people and places that are not written in English, but use a different character set as do Spanish and French with certain accent or punctuation marks not readily available in English.

The use of data servers is also a potential issue. At one extreme is the situation where the company providing the digitizing allows what is effectively a rental of its digitized data; that is, the data is kept on the company's server, and your users are granted access by what is, in effect, a proxy. Even a "sale" is presumed to be the ability for your organization to get access to the data forever, companies often go out of business, or get subsumed into other businesses, making a "sale" rather useless. The same difficulty can occur with a rental, because rental rates often go up.

Even if your organization is allowed to host the data on its own server, the company selling or renting the previously digitized data may also have contractual restrictions on the installation of a server in your organization on the number of concurrent users allowed access at any one time, or the number of users per day or per month, as well as the amount of data that can be downloaded.

Computers are much more reliable than in the past. However, they do not last forever. This is an issue that divides data providers and purchasers. If you purchase a license that states that the data can be hosted only on one server computer, what happens if the physical computer dies? Customer support may help with this problem, but companies may go out of business or be acquired, so your organization may have a long wait time, for reinstalling it. So your organization wants a backup or, at least, the ability to reinstall on a new system.

A data provider has other requirements, primarily the ability to make sure that its data is not stolen or misused. After all, the company providing the digitized data doesn't want to lose its assets. They might not trust the security of data stored on customer's servers and would thus want the data to be stored on their own, presumably secured, servers.

A final item to be considered is how the product will be delivered. This can be done purely over the Internet, provided that your organization's bandwidth is sufficient for the data transfer.

Alternatively, the data can be provided on a physical device, such as one or more portable USB drives. In view of the security concerns of the company providing the data, the portable drive may be locked to prevent copying.

In summary, the planning steps are:

1. Interact with representatives of potential providers of digitized data.
2. Develop plans for naming conventions of data.
3. Decide about location of data servers.
4. Decide about offering or requiring paywalls.
5. Create an installation plan.
6. Decide about backup of both servers and software.
7. Determine if the digital data will be stored and organized in a standard format or a proprietary one?
8. Determine if your organization will keep a minimal amount of the most basic microfilm and microfiche readers be provided to serve as a backup.
9. Determine if there any future obligations between the parties involved.

Economic Analysis of the Plan

Once the issues discussed in the section on planing have been addressed, it is possible to go forward with your economic assessment. You presumably have obtained initial quotes from several companies. You have a good understanding of the internal costs and logistics of going forward with digitization.

From one perspective, the most important remaining issues are the company you choose to work with and whether to buy or lease the product. Still, the economic issues may be the most pressing concern to your organization.

The economic analysis of the digitization effort must also include the cost of the local infrastructure improvement. This cost should be amortized over the cost of all current or planned digitization projects.

You will probably find is useful to use one of the appropriate Excel spreadsheets listed in the Appendix for economic analysis either as is, or as a guideline to developing one specifically designed for your own organization. These spreadsheets are available for free download.

Implementation of the Digitization Plan

We first consider the simplest possible case - the creation of an implementation plan to buy the digitized data.

Of course, the first step must be a search for companies that already have this data in a digital format and are willing to sell it at a reasonable cost. You may have done this search entirely on-line, or may have augmented it with information from conferences you or your colleagues attended, or even some informal information from others. There might be copies of the data that you wish to get that are freely available from the Internet, but the provider may be either not reliable or may not have rights to the data because the data was "pirated."

Assuming that you have completed this search, it is time to make a comparison As stated previously, I suggest you do this in the form of either a spreadsheet or some sort of project management software. Two simple *Microsoft Excel* spreadsheets, one with the companies' names in the top row and the other listing companies list in the left-most column can be downloaded freely at sites listed in the Appendix.

(Apple users should note that these spreadsheets will also run on Apple's *Numbers* software, since *Numbers* can import *Microsoft Excel* documents and save them in Excel format using the Export To option of the File menu. I have chosen to not include any specific project management software, because the most common basic project management software, *Microsoft Project*, is no longer included in the basic *Microsoft Office* distribution.)

Any spreadsheets you intend to use should contain the following fields (as do the spreadsheets mentioned above):

- Name of the company with the digitized data that you are considering to purchase.

- Complete address of the company, including website and physical location.

- Contact person or persons in charge of the transfer of the digitized data.

- Description of what precisely is being made available for the transfer.

- Description of how the digitized data will be distributed and whether the installation is to be done by your staff or the digitizing company.

- Date that the data is to be delivered.

- Cost of the digitized product.

- Does the company you are considering have the appropriate rights to transfer the original or a copy to your organization? Beware of bootleg copies.

- Reputation of the company, either by a respected source such as the Better Business Bureau, or by customer ratings.

- Written and/or online instructions for delivery.

- Do you have the ability to copy the digitized data as backup in case of a failure of your organization's servers?

- Do you have the ability to copy the digitized data if your organization has multiple locations that will have servers?

- Will your organization keep a minimal amount of the most basic microfilm and microfiche readers be provided to serve as a backup?

We next consider the implementation of an implementation plan for the situation in which your organization will lease the digitized data from a company.

The key difference here is that you will be entering a long-term relationship with a company. You must be very careful here to avoid potentially very large increases in annual rental fees. he contract probably should have options for purchase in the case that the company providing the digitized data is taken over by another company after a merger, or that the company decides to go out of the rental business entirely.

All other issues discussed in the spreadsheet mentioned above remain the same.

Post-Mortem Assessment

A serious port-mortem effort is your basic protection against any errors in the delivered product. It also can provide lessons learned for future digitization efforts. As was the case before in the previous sections on planning, economic analysis, and project management, basic spreadsheets intended to help with understanding this issue have been provided in the Appendix for free downloads.

The first questions to be considered for assessing the decision to buy the previously digitized data from a company are:

- Was the data provided on time?

- Was the data in the right format?

- Was the data of the high quality specified in the contract?

- Were the naming conventions followed?

- Did your organization keep a minimal amount of the most basic microfilm and microfiche readers be provided to serve as a backup?

- The most important question is, would you work with this company again?

As was the case previously, the first questions to be considered for assessing the decision to lease the previously digitized data from a company are:

- Was the data provided on time?

- Was the data in the right format?

- Was the data of the high quality specified in the contract?

- Were the naming conventions followed?

- Is the digital data continually available as needed?

- Will your organization keep a minimal amount of the most basic microfilm and microfiche readers be provided to serve as a backup?

- The most important question is, would you work with this company again?

Chapter 6. Use a Digitization Service

This chapter describes e\the use of a service to digitize your organization's microfilm and microfiche data instead of purchasing or leasing the same data from a remote source.

What to Expect

There are multiple considerations here, depending on whether the digitization is carried out on-site at your organization's location or remotely at a company's location.

If the digitization is done at the digitizing company's location, then you should expect the following:

- A schedule for the digitization to be completed must agree with the limits that have been specified in the contract.

- All of your organization's microfilm and microfiche submitted for digitization must be returned, and be delivered in a timely manner as specified in the contract.

- Any of your organization's microfilm or microfiche that is damaged during the digitization process should be repaired if possible, or replaced, otherwise.

- The digitized information must be transmitted and received in the manner specified in the contract.

- Naming conventions for file names must be provided in the manner specified in the instructions in the contract.

- The newly digitized data must be delivered in the agreed upon format.

• The newly created data should have no restrictions made on the ability of your organization to make copies for internal use or even external use if appropriate.

• The newly created data should have no restrictions to made on the ability of your organization to allow simultaneous users.

If the digitization is done at your own organization's location, then you should expect the following:

• A schedule for the digitization to be completed must agree with the limits specified in the contract.

• All of your organization's microfilm and microfiche submitted for digitization must be returned, and be delivered in a timely manner as specified in the contract.

• Any of your organization's microfilm or microfiche that is damaged during the digitization process should be repaired if possible, or replaced, otherwise.

• The digitized information must be transmitted and received in the manner specified in the contract.

• Naming conventions for file names must be provided in the manner specified in the instructions in the contract.

• The newly digitized data must be delivered in the agreed upon format.

• The newly created data should have no restrictions made on the ability of your organization to make copies for internal use or external use as appropriate.

• The newly created data should have no restrictions made on the ability of your organization to allow simultaneous users.

• If the digitization was done on-site using leased digitization equipment, the digitizing company must certify that this equipment was returned in good condition.

• If the digitization was done on-site using purchased digitization equipment, the digitizing company must certify that this equipment is still in good condition.

As you can see, there are different issues depending on whether the digitization is done on-site or remotely. We'll expand on this farther in the next section.

Two Very Different Options

The primary difference between the digitization processes described in this chapter and what was described in the previous one is that your organization will have less control of the microfilm and microfiche if you use the services of a company that provides digitization service. Depending on the options you choose, in some cases, you will have no control whatsoever of your data for the time that the data stored on your microfilm or microfiche will be under the physical control of the digitizing company. In other cases, your organization will retain guardianship of the physical media even during the process of its data as it being digitized at your organization's own site.

We will consider what at first glance appears to be the simplest option first. Your organization decides what it wants to digitize, what naming conventions and filename labeling it wishes to use, what the schedule is, and, of course, what the costs are. One or more classes of data, such as a complete run of a particular newspaper's issues for a ten-year period, or a set of records of political speeches of a local hero, may be given to the digitizing company. The whole process seems simple and should work well. Of course, your organization must have a copy of the microfilm and microfiche records it wants digitized as protection against fires, power failures, and even internal changes in the digitizing company. We'll discuss these issues of potential disasters later.

The advantages of having a company that specializes in digitization doing all their work at their own site, with well-maintained equipment and trained, highly experienced personnel are obvious.

In addition, the digitization effort may occur incrementally, with additional microfilm and microfiche data added to the digitization process as time and financial considerations warrant. (Sometimes it is a good idea to extend a project over several fiscal years for budgetary reasons.)

The disadvantage of having the digitization take place at a company's location is that your organization will lose physical control of its data at least temporarily. At first glance, it would seem that this is not a problem, but this may not be the case, as we will see in the next two paragraphs.

Next let's consider doing the scanning entirely at your organization's own location. A primary advantage of this choice is that you always maintain control of your organization's data, which is its own intellectual property. I personally prefer this approach because of an unfortunate situation that I had been told about when I was a young faculty member in the mathematics department.

A company asked to borrow my university library's extensive collection of the extremely important international journal of classical mathematics, *Mathematische Annalen*. The company said they would copy the contents to microfiche page by page, then return the original bound copies of the journal as well as a copy of the microfiche created. (This was prior to the digital age, so the copies would have been exact analog images, with no other searching possible.) As you can imagine from me discussing this disaster in this book, the company neither returned the bound volumes nor gave us a set of scanned copies of the journal issues on microfiche. Beware of losing your precious data!

Of course, if your organization does the scanning at its own location, the equipment and software to digitize must be either purchased or rented. There also must be a person who can perform the scanning. In most cases, a scanning service that rents equipment provides training for the person or persons on your organization's staff who will do the scanning.

On the other hand, if the scanning service provides their own personnel to work at your location, you should expect that the labor charge for the scanning will be much larger than if it were done at the scanning service's location. The scanning company will charge a considerable amount of overhead for this, with an additional amount for travel and living expenses if any of their out-of-town personnel is at your site. Training one or more of your organization's personnel clearly is much less expensive than using someone from the scanning company at your location.

A hybrid approach to digitization may be preferable at times. For example, your organization may arrange for the digitization equipment to be set up at your organization's site by personnel of the digitization company and a first set of digitization of a microfilm tape may be done by that company's personnel. This might be followed by the digitization of a second tape by organizational staff under the tutelage of a company employee, followed by perhaps a final digitization. In any case, the costs of such a hybrid service should be made clear in the contract. It may happen, of course, that this transition is too abrupt and additional training is required, probably at extra cost.

Planning for Digitization

As we did in Chapter 5, we will discuss the issues with both the essentially turnkey and internally performed digitization service in the same sections in this chapter, with the simpler case of contracting for turnkey service discussed first and the additional issues specific to the situation of a more extended relationship for the service discussed at a later time.

The search for digitizing companies should be limited to companies with relatively local technical support staff. Travel can be expensive and multiple visits can be time and resource consuming. Ideally, you will be able to consult the company's references.

It cannot be emphasized enough. If your organization chooses to buy the digitization service and give up temporary control of its intellectual property assets, it is essential that a copy of any microfilm or microfiche that is to be digitized must be made before relinquishing control to that company for any length of time, in order to prevent against disaster.

Here are the issues that must be decided on during the planning process:

- What is the reputation of the digitization company?

- What are the time constraints for digitization?

- Will all digitization work be done remotely at the location of the digitization company or locally?

- If the digitization is to be done at your location, will you purchase or lease the digitization equipment?

- Does the digitizing company have room in its schedule for the hardware, software, and trained digitizers that your digitization effort needs?

- If the digitizing company does not have all these resources available in a timely manner, is there a backup plan?

- Will your organization's staff be trained in proper digitization?

As stated above, one of the first steps in the planning process is determining if your organization wishes to purchase or lease the digitization equipment. Both options have advantages and disadvantages.

Buying digitization equipment means that the equipment will always be available to your organization, which may decide to digitize its records incrementally. It may make it easier to allocate staffing resources in so-called slack times. Keep in mind that equipment and software may become obsolete over a period of time.

Leasing the equipment will have lower up-front costs, but may not be well-suited to organizational needs if there is a large number of distinct sets of records to be digitized and the process will take along time. This approach may be more expensive in total, but can avoid trying to use hardware and software that is no longer supported on a local computer's operating system

Your organization should limit its search to companies that sell such equipment to those that provide at least training manuals and on-line tutorials. Training courses may be offered at a company site, or may be available at your site, although probably at a higher cost.

Economic Analysis of the Plan

Let's consider the costs of what we could call "buying the service;" that is, having the digitization company provide its service at its own location using its own equipment on your own data that is currently stored on microfilm or microfiche. Not surprisingly, this is a relatively simple situation. As before, links to a *Microsoft Excel* spreadsheet to help in your analysis can be downloaded in the Appendix.

Here is an example of the unexpected technical requirements of a digitizing system that can be rented by an archive. The technology is accurate as of the time this book is being written. However, in the interest of fairness and professionalism, I suggest you contact vendors directly for the latest technology requirements and pricing.

You might think that the company providing the digitization service would use commodity computers to handle the digitization. Unfortunately, this might not be true. One company I had worked with on a digitization project had very specific requirements for the powerful PC needed to run it's software in terms of its internal power supply and the ability to have multiple USB connections in order to be able to connect multiple USB disks and the scanner, itself. Such powerful PCs are rarely available at your neighborhood retailer. Since I do not do any heavy computational work on my Macs at home, I am not aware of any such powerful Macs that accommodate these needs. Do your own research if necessary if your organization uses Macs.

Here are the costs to consider:

- Creation of backup copies of all microfilm or microfiche to be digitized.

- Contract for specific services to be performed, including using naming conventions for creating and using file names.

- Cost of labor at the digitizing company.

- Cost of using the machines doing the digitization. This is probably incorporated together with the charge for labor in the contract.

- Format of the delivery of the digitized data.

- Return of all analog copies (microfilm reels and microfiche) to your organization after digitization is complete.

Many of the cost factors listed above for having the digitization done entirely at the digitizing organization's site also occur if the digitization is to be done in house by leasing equipment to use at your site, as opposed to buying equipment to use at your site.

Here are the costs to consider:

- Creation of backup copies of all microfilm or microfiche to be digitized.

- Contract for specific services to be performed, including using naming conventions for creating and using file names.

- Cost of labor from the digitizing company for the services of trainers and the initial digitizers.

- Cost of labor at your organization. Thus may be an actual cost, or the effective cost of some other work that your organization does regularly, but may have to be postponed due to staff being assigned to digitization.

- Cost of buying the machines doing the digitization.

- Cost of renting the machines doing the digitization. (This option is not very common because some digitization companies may be concerned about having their own intellectual property being reverse engineered.)

- Format of the delivered version of the digitized data.

- Return of all analog copies (microfilm reels and microfiche sheets) to your organization's storage facility after digitization is complete.

Implementation of the Digitization Plan

The implementation plan for a project which will have all an organization's digitization done at the digitizing company is relatively simple. It is based on the availability of funds at your organization, and available resources at the digitizing company.

The situation is not so simple if the work is being done remotely at your organization instead.

Since there must be close coordination of schedules between your organization and the digitizing company, the project plan for digitization must be carefully thought out. It is even more complicated if the work is scheduled to take place in multiple phases over a long period.

Post-Mortem Assessment

In Chapter 5, we recommended doing a post-mortem at the completion of the digitization. If the digitization is done completely by the digitizing company at its own site, it seems natural that the post-mortem should be done at the end of the digitization.

Unfortunately, if the digitization is done using purchased or rented hardware and equipment, whether entirely by external staff, internal staff, or a combination thereof, it is natural suggest that post-mortem assessments are done not just at the end of the entire digitization project, but at the end of each phase. One obvious added transition point is the transition from an employee of the digitizing company doing the digitization to having it done by an employee of your organization who is working under the watchful eye of an expert. A second transition point might be when one or more of your employees who have been trained by the company expert are able to do the work on their own, without supervision.

As before, the most important question is, would you work with this company again?

Chapter 7. Do-It-Yourself Low-Cost Digitization

The do-it-yourself digitization processes that we will describe in this chapter have a tremendous advantage over the processes that were described in Chapter 6 in the sense that the valuable data on your organization's microfilm and microfiche media never leave your organization's control, or, at least, never leave the control of a volunteer working under the auspices of a staff member. The risk of this on-site approach is limited to possible physical damage to the physical media that holds your data.

There are three primary disadvantages to this type of approach.

1. The procedure we suggest here is extremely time-consuming.
2. Data may not be available during the digitization process in any convenient service location.
3. There are quality control issues, because not all of the people doing the digitizing will be trained professional staff; many will be volunteers.

It is very important to have some procedural mechanism in place to make sure all the volunteers perform their work to the standards that the organization has created.

Finally, there is an additional cost of do-it-yourself digitization that may not be obvious at first glance. The staff members will undoubtably require training to be able to use the digitizing equipment properly. Volunteers will, of course, need even more training, especially in ethical issues.

There is an extreme case of low-cost do-it-yourself digitization that can best be categorized as being "citizen science." This term is generally used to describe such applications as geographically separated amateurs collecting rainfall and temperature data and reporting it, or by reading multiple photographs of astronomical regions and determining if there are exoplanets orbiting distant stars by deciding if stars have been partially occluded by an exoplanet.

I'll describe two such citizen science projects in this chapter, one wildly successful and one that never got beyond the initial planning stages.

The wildly successful citizen science digitization project took place at the Maryland State Archives in Annapolis. An organization called "Reclaim the Records," with the website reclaimtherecords.org[1] has the goal of making genealogical records publicly available without requiring paywalls such as are created by ancestry.com[2] and myheritage.com[3]. This organization worked hand-in-hand with the Maryland State Archives to make sets of records that had already been scanned by the archives available but originally intended only for use via microfilm at the archive building become digitally available to all, and to store them at the free site, archive.org[4]. In some cases, material had to be redacted due to privacy concerns. (Some marriage records included Social Security Numbers of the bride and groom.) This was a large cooperative effort! The stellar reputation of Reclaim the Records was essential in this effort.

A citizen science digitization effort that never got off the ground was aimed at a collection of ethnic newspapers at a local historical society museum. The idea was to have dozens of volunteers photograph each page, then combine the page images into PDF files for each issue. The project was scrapped when it was clear that there was little room to have more than two people at a time in an area with room to lay large newspaper pages flat and set up tripods for cameras. The project never even got to the point where the proper lighting for cameras was considered. Using cell phone cameras was not a solution.

We will not consider digitization of microfilm or microfiche by citizen science processes any farther in this book and will focus on your organization using more coordinated techniques.

What to Expect

Let's suppose that your organization has one or more reels of microfilm or microfiche that is wishes to digitize. Suppose that the methods suggested in the

---

1.   http://reclaimtherecords.org

2.   http://ancestry.com

3.   http://myheritage.com

4.   http://archive.org

last two chapters are deemed too expensive for the organization's discretionary budget. Is there anything that can be done to digitize some microfilm and free up underutilized space? I'll describe briefly a solution that I could work with several years ago that I'll describe below. (There is a caveat, however — equipment and software are often updated, and usage policies may change.)

Fortunately there is a low-cost method, at least in some situations. When faced with the aforementioned cost issues, in terms of buying or leasing a digitization service, the organization I was volunteering with wanted another solution. I was told about a particular location of a Family History Center of a Later Day Saints (Mormon) church. Since the Mormons place such importance with genealogical research locations are always available to the public for non-commercial use without any religious pressure.

I was informed that this particular location, co-located with a Temple in the Washington, DC area had a very high-quality microfilm reader with a smooth connection to a high-resolution printer.This equipment, while not automated, was much faster and produced much better images than the equipment at any of the closer local Family History Centers in the Baltimore, Maryland area.

I drove to the larger Family History Center in Washington, using back roads instead of the DC Beltway to make the drive unpleasant instead of intolerable. I would get to the Center at about opening time, reserve one of the three high-quality microfilm readers, pay a small hourly fee, insert a USB flash drive and start to copy images, one at a time. A boring job, and I learned that, since there was no inexpensive and fast restaurant nearby, to pack a lunch and eat in my car in the parking lot. I found that it was best to end up before a rush of younger users came in, in order to concentrate on the job at hand. Besides, it was better to leave early enough to avoid the terrible traffic going home.

I was able to digitize images for an entire ten-year run of an ethnic newspaper at essentially no cost. Would I have done this for a much longer run of newspapers? Probably not.

One other thing needs mentioning. One day, I had forgotten to bring a flash drive. The Family History Center sold me an inexpensive one with large enough capacity to copy a day's work of digitizing images.

What will your experience with such a process be?

- The equipment will be better at producing high-quality images than the ones usually used, and faster, too.

- There may be restrictions in how long you can use these machines each day.

- There may be restrictions on how many images you can digitize each day.

- There may be ways to use more high-quality, and more automated, equipment than what is typically available to the general public. This would certainly require at least a letter of support from your organization that assures that the digitized media will not be sold or leased. Other permissions may be necessary.

- There may be other places besides local Family History Centers that have microfilm readers that can digitize images.

Planning for Digitization

The first step in this type of digitization process is to determine which nearby locations have microfilm readers that can digitize images. Do an expansive search, not necessarily limiting your search to Family History Centers. Once you have done this, the planning process can proceed.

- Get as many volunteers as you can.

- Determine how many hours they are likely to commit to working on this effort.

- Develop a plan for allocation of volunteers to machines.

- Keep volunteers happy by having machines available when they arrive. This requires coordination.

• Create a written set of instructions.

• Determine how to break up the amount of data that each volunteer will be asked to digitize. Try to make sure that no particular run of data is split between two or more volunteers.

• Keep an accurate record of what has been digitized and who did the digitization and where.

• Make sure that each volunteer signs out the microfilm they will take each day they work.

• Make sure that each volunteer returns the microfilm when completed.

• This one is tricky. Be certain to get permissions from your organization's officers to do the digitization. You may not need this at any digitization site. However, keep in mind that it is often easier to ask for forgiveness than to ask for permission.

• Make sure the volunteers are rewarded, at least by recognition in some written document, and, perhaps, by a small party.

Economic Analysis of the Plan

As is usual, we'll start with a discussion of purchasing the digitization equipment. The costs to digitize microfilm are:

• Purchase of the hardware needed to digitize microfilm data. This includes the costs of any peripherals.

• Purchase of the software needed to digitize microfilm data.

• Purchase of any training materials needed to digitize microfilm.

• Purchase of licenses to use for digitization of microfilm data.

The costs to digitize microfiche are similar to those for digitizing microfilm:

• Purchase of the hardware needed to digitize microfiche data. This includes the costs of any peripherals.

• Purchase of the software needed to digitize microfiche data.

• Purchase of any training materials needed to digitize microfiche.

• Purchase of licenses to use for digitization of microfiche data.

As before, links to an Excel spreadsheet for keeping track of this approach are included in the Appendix.

Implementation of the Digitization Plan

This type of plan should be developed incrementally. As a first step, a single roll of microfilm or sheet of microfiche should be digitized and the resulting set of digitized images should be evaluated for quality and for the efficiency of the digitization process.

Once this assessment of the initial digitization effort has been evaluated and found to be of adequate quality, and any changes in the originally designed process have been determined and instituted, the digitization may proceed.

Post-Mortem Assessment

Since the digitization process is incremental, the post-mortem assessment of the process will be replaced largely by assessments of the results after each stage of digitization.

Of course, there will be at least a small overall post-mortem assessment after the entire digitization is completed.

Get post-mortem input from your volunteers in both formal and informal ways.

Chapter 8. How to Delay Digital Obsolescence

Of course, it is impossible to delay the march of technological advancement. It is almost as difficult to appreciate the importance of many technical advances at the time they occur. Here are two examples, one you might of heard and one that is almost certainly not known to you, at least not until you read this book.

Bill Gates famously admitted that he had underestimated the importance of the Internet! He soon changed his viewpoint and now a Microsoft product, *Microsoft Office*, has become currently available only as a primarily web-based version.

In the early-to-mid 1990s, well before the C++ programming language was standardized, I told one of my software engineering classes that object-oriented programming was a fad and would become a cottage industry. I soon changed my view, seeing the value of such things as the APIs (Application Programming Interfaces) that permeate so much software development on smart phones and nearly all personal computers. I even wrote a book on object-oriented programming!

What percentage of the readers of this book are reading it on a phone? That would have been unheard of about twenty-five years ago.

Standardizing Data Formats

Clearly, there will be changes in technology during the life span of your newly digitized data. Some common devices will become smaller and more portable, and some hardware interfaces will change. Just look at how connections to iPhones have changed, making charging cables obsolete. The new movement to the USB-C standard is the result of a push from standards organizations. Expect future changes.

Your organization may have had to react to changes in the way that microfilm readers have changed over time, with new standards for connecting cables.

So, change is inevitable. What can your organization do? Your organization can make sure that any digitized data you have uses the same standard, recognizing that any changes in digital display technology can either be overlooked because any new display technology should be backward compatible with what you have. This standardization gives you two possible approaches to protecting against obsolescence.

Your organization's first, and best, defense against technological advances making images difficult or impossible to read in the future is by making sure that the images are stored in a single format, ideally the most likely to be supported in the future. What about standards for digital image data? There are lots of formats that can be used to store digital images. For example, there are many formats that a simple screen shot created on a Macintosh computer can be exported to: HEIC, JPG, JPG-2000, OpenEXR, PDF, PNG, and TIFF. A file whose name has a .JPG or .jpg extension is a JPG file, using a standard of the *Joint Photographic Group*, and other file name extensions refer to other standards.

Nearly all these formats have been standardized to some degree either by a standards organization or by a software company. The standardization process may have been international in scope.

The standards may have been set up to minimize the number of bytes needed for storage by compressing the images, with software decompressing the image data file to allow it to be displayed on a screen.

Other graphical formats, such as PNG, allow the ability to edit a graphical image file. This capability is automatically available for free on a Mac, or by products from Adobe and others. I don't think the ability to make edits is appropriate for any images where the original images stored on microfilm or microfiche is considered to be as authoritative as the original document (which may have been on paper.). We note that for genealogical and archival purposes, microfilm images of the United States Census are considered to be as reliable as the original paper documents.

There is one other data image format that you may encounter, the bitmap. Bitmap files have a .BMP or .bmp extension. Bitmap files are stored as collections of pixels, the little dots that make up images that are shown on a screen. Bitmap image files can be either black-and-white or in color. We will discuss each of the options for the storage of bitmap images briefly.

Each pixel in a black-and-white image can be represented by a single right-bit byte. This means a range of 00000000 to 1111111 can be stored, providing a gray-scale of 256 options. (If the file represents a purely black-and-white image, with no gray-scales included, only one bit of each byte may be necessary. This option, which might work well for simple newsletters and newspapers, is not commonly available on modern computers.)

A color image is more complicated. Many older computer graphics systems use red, green, blue standard, for the specification of colors in each pixel, where three bytes are used on the same 00000000 to 11111111 scale for each of the three aforementioned primary colors. Thus, there could be 256 gradations of each of these colors in a single pixel.

Newer systems, particularly high end ones, may use two bytes for each color in a pixel. This means 65,336 possibilities for each color in the scale. It is unlikely that this number will ever be exceeded due to limitations of human vision!

Converting Data Formats

A second level of protection against this obsolescence is that there is a huge amount of digital image data available now in a huge number of institutional and other servers. If you have become a victim of a large change in technology, and your data is no longer accessible to your organization, there are other organizations that have the same problem. Market forces and the creativity of entrepreneurs make it extremely likely that graphical image formats will have converter software available.

Warning — there is some technical computer code presented in the remainder of this section, which is fortunately the last material included in the body of this book. If you do read it, use it to try to understand what a person who is well-versed in such code is actually doing, rather than expecting to do the programming yourself.

Programs to convert files from one form to another are readily available on the Internet. At the present time these converter programs are very likely to be free, but there are also commercial programs.

These programs are rarely in the form of apps that can be downloaded in the app stores associated with iPhones or Android phones. Typically, they are designed in to be used within a terminal window because that allows the conversion of many files from one data format to another with a few lines of code.

Terminal windows are available on both a Mac and on a PC. You might remember using the C:> prompt in early versions of MS-DOS. Terminal windows are also available on computers running on many versions of Linux.

An image of the small icon on my Mac that is used to open a terminal window looks like the one shown below:

The advantage of a terminal window is that is can allow what are known as shell commands to be entered and executed. Let's look at what might happen if someone enters the following shell command

converter < old_data_file > new_data_file

I have shown a small terminal window indicating how the shell command is entered at the shell prompt (which is my user login name) on this computer.

```
Rons-New-Air:~ ronaldjleach$
Rons-New-Air:~ ronaldjleach$
Rons-New-Air:~ ronaldjleach$
Rons-New-Air:~ ronaldjleach$
Rons-New-Air:~ ronaldjleach$
Rons-New-Air:~ ronaldjleach$
Rons-New-Air:~ ronaldjleach$
Rons-New-Air:~ ronaldjleach$
Rons-New-Air:~ ronaldjleach$
Rons-New-Air:~ ronaldjleach$
Rons-New-Air:~ ronaldjleach$ converter < old_data_file  > new_data_file[]
```

Here's how the above line of code is interpreted. There are separate entities on this command line:

1. *converter* is the name of the program to be executed.
2. The less-than sign, <, means that the program named converter is to get its input from a file that is identified in the next symbol.
3. *old_data_file* is the name of an existing data file whose contents are to be converted.
4. The greater-than sign, >, indicates that the output of this conversion is to be placed into a file that is identified in the next symbol.
5. *new_data_file* is the name of the file that is the result of this conversion.
6. The [] is simply a prompt that says that a new command can be entered.

If there are, say twelve files to be converted, representing a year's worth of newspaper, a shell script such as the one below might be necessary

```
for index in 1 to 12
    do
    converter < old_data_file$index > new_data_file$index
    done
```

Here the term "index" is used to indicate that it represents an index that distinguishes different file names. The $ sign indicates that the value of the index is to be used and not its name. These four lines of code are equivalent to the twelve lines

```
converter < old_data_file1 > new_data_file1
    converter < old_data_file2 > new_data_file2
    ...
    converter < old_data_file12 > new_data_file12
```

Even if you do not understand this code example, notice that there ways that some (perhaps unknown) technical expert who would be able to provide some levels of protection against technological obsolescence.

Appendix. Downloadable Spreadsheets

The following spreadsheets are available for free download from either of the author's websites www.rleach.com/spreadsheets/Microfilm[1] or distance-college.com/spreadsheets/Microfilm[2]. Those readers who have selected the print version of this book instead of the ebook version should use this prefix followed by the spreadsheets indicated below. Feel free to modify or share these spreadsheets as appropriate.

For Chapter 5 spreadsheets, look for:

- Planning spreadsheet for purchasing already digitized data: *Chap5PlanPurchaseDigitizedData.xlsx*.

- Project management spreadsheet for purchasing already digitized data: *Chap5ProjectManagementPlan.xlsx*.

- Post-mortem spreadsheet for purchasing already digitized data: *Chap5Post-Mortem.xlsx*.

For Chapter 6 spreadsheets, look for:

- Planning spreadsheet for leasing already digitized data: *Chap6Plan.xlsx*. xxx names of the next two

- Economic plan spreadsheet for leasing already digitized data.

- Project management spreadsheet for leasing already digitized data.

- Post-mortem spreadsheet for leasing already digitized data.

---

1. http://www.rleach.com/spreadsheets/Microfilm

2. http://distance-college.com/spreadsheets/Microfilm

Disclaimer:

All images in this book are in the public domain and are freely available from Wikimedia Commons, the National Archives, or from the Library of Congress.

Also by Ronald J. Leach

Software Reuse: Methods, Models, Costs, Second Edition
Why 2K?
Where Have All The Templars Gone?
User Guide to Microfilm and Microfiche
The 101 Most Important UNIX and Linux Commands
Baltimore Blue and Freddie Gray
Digitizing Microfilm and Microfiche
Managing a Digital Estate Without Paper Records

About the Author

About the Author

I recently retired from being a professor of computer science at **Howard University** for over 25 years, with 9 of those years as a department chair. (I was a math professor for 16 years before that.) While I was department chair, we sent more students to work at Microsoft in the 2004-5 academic year than any other college or university in the United States. We also established a graduate certificate program in computer security, which became the largest certificate program at the university. I had major responsibility for working with technical personnel to keep our department's hundreds of computers functional and virus-free, while providing email service to several hundred users. We had to withstand constant hacker attacks and we learned how to reduce the vulnerability of our computer systems.

As a scholar/researcher, I studied complex computer systems and their behavior when attacked or faced with heavy, unexpected loads. I wrote five books on computing, from particular programming languages, to the internal structure of sophisticated operating systems, to the development and efficient creation of highly complex applications. My long-term experience with computers (I had my first computer programming course in 1964) has helped me understand the nature of many of the computer attacks by potential identity thieves and, I hope, be able to explain them and how to defend against them, to a general audience of non-specialists. More than 5,000 people have attended my lectures on identity theft; many others have seen them on closed-circuit television.

I have written more than twenty books, and more than 120 technical articles, most of which are in technical areas.

My interests in data storage and access meshed well with my genealogical interests when I wrote the Genealogy Technology column of the **Maryland Genealogical Society Journal** for several years. I was the editor or co-editor of that society's journal for many years.

About the Publisher

AfterMath is a small, highly selective publisher based in Baltimore, Maryland, focusing on high-quality technical books and selected thoughtfully written fiction.